The Parable of the Prodigal Son: Rebellion, Repentance, Restoration, Rejection, and Reward

Barry A. Allen

Copyright © 2018 Barry Alexander Allen

All rights reserved.

ISBN-10: 1979693471

ISBN-13: 978-1979693479

All Scripture references are from the

King James Version of the Bible

For Mom,
Mrs. Sarah Lee Holland Allen,
of Johnston County, North Carolina,
We Truly are Champions,
Thanks to Jesus and You

Contents

PART I – REBELLION 9

PART II – REPENTANCE 23

PART III – RESTORATION 43

PART IV – REJECTION 65

PART V – REWARD 87

The Parable of the Prodigal Son

Luke 15:11-32 – "And he said, a certain man had two sons: And the younger of them said to his father, Father, give me the portion of goods that falleth to me. And he divided unto them his living. And not many days after the younger son gathered all together, and took his journey into a far country, and there wasted his substance with riotous living. And when he had spent all, there arose a mighty famine in that land; and he began to be in want. And he went and joined himself to a citizen of that country; and he sent him into his fields to feed swine. And he would fain had filled his belly with the husks that the swine did eat: and no man gave unto him. And when he came to himself, he said, How many hired servants of my father's have bread enough and to spare, and I perish with hunger! I will arise and go to my father, and will say unto him, Father, I have sinned against heaven, and before thee, And am no more worthy to be called thy son: make me as one of thy hired servants. And he arose, and came to his father. But when he was yet a great way off, his father saw him, and had compassion, and ran, and fell on his neck, and kissed him. And the son said unto him, Father, I have sinned against heaven, and in thy sight, and am no more worthy to be called thy son. But the father said to his servants, Bring forth the best robe, and put it on him; and put a ring on his hand, and shoes on his feet: And bring hither the fatted calf, and kill it; and let us eat, and be merry: For this my son was dead, and is alive again; he was lost, and is found. And they began to be merry. Now his elder son was in the field: and as he came and drew nigh to the house, he heard musick and dancing. And he called one of the servants, and asked what these things meant. And he said unto him, Thy brother is come; and thy father hath killed the fatted calf, because he hath received him safe and sound. And he was angry, and would not go in: therefore came his father out, and intreated him. And he answering said to his father, Lo, these many years do I serve thee, neither transgressed I at any time thy commandment: and yet thou never gavest me a kid, that I might make merry with my friends: But as soon as this thy son was come, which hath devoured thy living with harlots, thou hast killed for him the fatted calf. And he said unto him, Son, thou art ever with me, and all that I have is thine. It was meet that we should make merry, and be glad: for this thy brother was dead, and is alive again; and was lost, and is found."

PART I – REBELLION

Chapter 1 – Losing Focus

Luke 15:11-13

"And he said, A certain man had two sons: And the younger of them said to his father, Father give me the portion of goods that falleth to me. And he divided unto them his living. And not many days after the younger son gathered all together, and took his journey into a far country, and there wasted his substance with riotous living."

Ingratitude, Temptation, and the Allure of Far Away Lands

The Parable of the Prodigal Son is one of the greatest stories ever told. We Christians love it because it is so very rich in theological truth, and we can relate to the young man in so many ways. We realize that we all have sinned in our lives both prior to and after our conversions. We see ourselves in the story, and we see our loving God in the story as well. So, it is a story about us and God and how God receives sinners back home when they turn from their sin and come back home to their Father. This makes this story hit very close to home every time we read, study, reflect, teach, preach, or hear a sermon or lesson taught on the Parable of the Prodigal Son. It is a glorious story which reminds us of the dangers of sin, the cost of sin, and the consequences of sin. And, it also reminds us that we always have the opportunity to repent, and turn away from our sin, and begin our journey back home to our God, who loves us, waits for us, runs to embrace us, and throws a great celebration for us when we arrive back home at our heavenly Father's house.

When We Take Things for Granted

The son had everything he could ever want at his father's house. He had good food to eat, a roof over his head, and a loving family. Why would he set his eyes upon a foreign land? Why would he ask for his inheritance so that he could leave and go live a wild lifestyle in a land that he knew not of? The grass may be greener on the other side of the hill, but we must remember that the greener grass oftentimes grows over the septic tank.

In the Parable of the Prodigal Son, we see many aspects of God's nature and man's nature. Here, in the beginning of the Parable, we see that "The heart is deceitful above all things, and desperately wicked: who can know it?" (Jeremiah 17:9) Man is seldom satisfied with what God provides but frequently searches and seeks more and more. This is the sinful reality of the human condition. We are coveting creatures. One of the most broken of the

Ten Commandments is the Tenth Commandment: "Thou shalt not covet..." (Exodus 20:17) As sinful creatures, we tend to want more and more, and our flesh is rarely fulfilled and completely satisfied. This is why the Scriptures teach us not to strive to fulfill the desires of the flesh because the flesh is rarely satisfied. Attempting to fulfill the desires of the flesh is like trying to shoot fish in a barrel or trying to quench one's thirst by drinking ocean water.

When we covet something that someone else has, we are not giving thanks for and appreciating what we have. This is what makes coveting such a serious sin. It is rooted and grounded in ingratitude. We should not take God's many blessings that he showers upon us for granted. The person who looks at and wants what another person has, and does not focus on and give thanks for what he has, is breaking the Tenth Commandment and coveting. This is a very serious sin which brings very serious consequences.

This is the sin that the younger son falls into in the Parable of the Prodigal Son. He listens to his flesh which tells him that he is not fulfilled in his father's house. He takes his eyes off all the many blessings he has and the fact that he has everything he could ever need right there at home. And, he sets his eyes upon a foreign land which, in reality, has nothing he truly needs just things and experiences that his sinful flesh desires. Unfortunately, as frail humans sometimes do, he listens to his flesh and makes the decision to request his inheritance so that he can answer the call of his flesh to go to this foreign and sinful land. In this distant land, the son will be separated from his father and his father's house. It will be an experience which will remind him of the security, love, comfort, and peace that he gave up when he left his father's house. He answered the call of his flesh to go to a distant land to engage in sin and squander his inheritance, and it was a mistake which costs him dearly but teaches him a priceless lesson.

Temptation and the Lust of the Eyes

When we look at the temptation of Christ in Matthew 4:1-11 and Luke 4:1-13, we see that the devil "shows" Jesus the things that he uses to tempt Jesus. This reminds us that the enemy often appeals to our senses, especially the sense of sight, when tempting us to disobey God and sin. We need to always keep in mind that "All That Glitters Is Not

Gold" and just because something looks good doesn't mean it is good. Things can "look" good but in actuality be "really" bad. We need to be on guard and prepared to avoid giving in to the desires of the flesh prompted by things that are pleasing to our eyes. The apostle John tells us in 1 John 2:15-17:

> Love not the world, neither the things that are in the world. If any man love the world, the love of the Father is not in him. For all that is in the world, the lust of the flesh, the lust of the eyes, and the pride of life, is not of the Father, but is of the world. And the world passeth away, and the lust thereof: but he that doeth the will of God abideth for ever.

We are not to follow what is pleasing to the eyes, but we are to follow what is pleasing to the Spirit. We are to follow Christ, his teachings, and his example. He lived a life of sacrifice, service, and he faithfully answered the call of his Father. We too are to answer the call of God in our lives, and we are not to answer the call of the flesh. It is important to remember the call of the flesh is not just in the arena of sensuality but also includes the temptation to commit other sins of the flesh like hatred, resentment, materialism, gluttony, greed, self-righteousness, religious superiority, racism, unforgiveness, discontent, and covetousness to name a few.

The younger son in the Parable of the Prodigal Son answers the call of his sinful flesh to go to a distant land, and he engages in the sinful activity which is prominent in that land. This leaves him separated from his father and his father's house. It costs him his inheritance, but he learns a very valuable lesson from the experience. In this great Parable, we are reminded that our God is indeed more than able to take the lemons in our lives and make delicious thirst-quenching lemonade. As we continue our study of this great story, we will see the good that comes to the younger son, and the entire family, as God works within and through these events.

In the Lord's Prayer in Matthew 6:10, we pray: "…lead us not into temptation, but deliver us from evil:…" Many are confused as to what this part of the Lord's Prayer is all about, but we see here in the Parable of the Prodigal Son exactly how it applies in the lives of Christians. We are simply asking God to help us not answer the call of the flesh which leads us in the way of sin. We are asking God to lead us in the ways of holiness and to help us resist giving in to the desires of the flesh and the temptations that come from the enemy. God doesn't lead persons into temptation, but we choose sin when we choose to give in to "…the lust of the flesh, and the lust of the eyes, and the pride of life,…" (1 John 2:16) If we consistently choose sin, we too will be separated from our Father's house, our spiritual inheritance, and our Father's presence. And, we too will find ourselves "feeding pigs" in a "foreign land."

The Parable of the Prodigal Son is a cautionary tale about the allure of sin and the price it demands. We need to remember that sin will always take us farther than we want to go, keep us longer than we want to stay, and cost us more than we want to pay. We learn from the Parable of the Prodigal Son that the foreign land the devil shows us is not where we want to be. We want to be in our Father's house, where "…goodness and mercy shall follow [us] all the days of [our lives], and [we] will dwell in the house of the Lord for ever" (Psalm 23:6). We should never take for granted all the blessings of being obedient Christians. The joy of radical obedience is unparalleled with anything this world can offer. The man or woman who kneels before God can stand before anyone. And, when we know we are right with God, we can face anything this world throws at us, and we can face it with courage and unwavering faith remembering that Jesus says: "…In the world ye shall have tribulation: but be of good cheer; I have overcome the world" (John 16:33).

PART II – REPENTANCE

Chapter 2 – Coming to Our Senses

Luke 15:15-19 – "And he went and joined himself to a citizen of that country; and he sent him into his fields to feed swine. And he would fain have filled his belly with the husks that the swine did eat: and no man gave unto him. And when he came to himself, he said, How many hired servants of my father's have bread enough and to spare, and I perish with hunger! I will arise and go to my father, and will say unto him, Father, I have sinned against heaven, and before thee. And am no more worthy to be called thy son: make me as one of thy hired servants."

Confessing Our Sins and Changing Directions

The younger son is not in the foreign country long before he runs through all of his money. The party lifestyle is very expensive, and one tends to have plenty of fun and friends as long as he or she is buying. However, when the money runs out, and the parties are all over, then we tend to find out who our friends really are. We detect this reality in our Parable in v.15. In v. 15, we read: "And he went and joined himself to a citizen of that country; and he sent him into his fields to feed swine." When he arrived in the foreign land, the Prodigal Son had plenty of money, and this probably allowed him to make plenty of friends. He was so popular that he was able to "join himself" to a citizen of the distant land, and this person was probably one of his primary party friends. He allowed the Prodigal Son to live in his house because the Prodigal Son was financing good times with food, strong drink, and ladies to the left and to the right. It is not too much of a stretch to think that the young man's host may have also convinced him to finance repairs to his home, purchase new livestock, or provide food and clothing for himself and his family. The result would be that the Prodigal Son's large inheritance would diminish even more rapidly if his host was sinfully taking advantage of his young and gullible tenant.

It was as if the fun would never end, but it always does. The younger son's inheritance eventually runs out, and a great famine occurs in the land. Now, the parties have ended and everyone is fending for him or herself. After all the young man did for his host, you would think that the host would allow the Prodigal Son to have a respectable position working on his estate. However, men and women tend to be quite ungrateful creatures, and sinners who have not been molded and shaped by God's Word, Commandments, and the Holy Spirit have a propensity and tendency to lean in the direction of selfishness, ingratitude, and plain old meanness.

Surprisingly, the host does give the Prodigal Son a job, but the pay is so little that the young man is literally starving. He is given a job feeding pigs which is particularly humiliating and even religiously "unclean" for a young Jewish man like the Prodigal Son. Jews are not to touch or consume swine, and this is made very clear in Leviticus 11:7-8 where we read:

> And the swine, though he divide the hoof, and be cloven-footed, yet he cheweth not the cud: he is unclean to you. Of their flesh shall ye not eat, and their carcase shall ye not touch; they are unclean to you.

Ironically, God allows the Prodigal Son to find himself in this particularly humiliating and religiously precarious situation. Of course, this reminds us that, although he is in a foreign land, far from where he should be in his father's house, the young man is not far from his heavenly Father who is speaking through this ordinary event of a young, sinful, and broken man carrying out the ordinary mundane chore of a farm-worker feeding the farmer's pigs.

This reminds us that our God loves sinners and prodigal sons and daughters. He never leaves them, and he even goes with them into the dangerous and dirty foreign lands that sinners and prodigals run to. We see God's great love for sinners throughout the Bible, and we see it in the other two powerful parables found in Chapter 15 of Luke's Gospel. This makes Luke 15 one of the most beautiful, amazing, powerful, and lovely chapters in the Bible. When a sinner repents and returns home to God, God is like the shepherd who leaves the 99 sheep and celebrates finding the 1 that was lost. (Luke 15:3-7) And, God is like the woman who loses a precious coin and searches diligently and sweeps the entire house and calls her friends to celebrate with her when she finds it. (Luke 15:8-10) So, our loving God, goes with sinners into those wretched lands of alcoholism, drug addiction, immorality, unforgiveness, hatred, pride, selfishness, and greed, and he continues to work through the events in the lives of sinners to remind them that there is still a way home. It is never too late. God continues to love, and he continues to care. He continues to long for the return of prodigal sons and daughters, and he continues to love sinners and offer them forgiveness if they will simply repent and return home to him.

As he feeds the pigs, the young man looks at the husks that they are eating and wishes he could have them. He is so hungry that he wants what the pigs are eating. In v. 16, we read: "And he would fain have filled his belly with the husks that the swine did eat; and no man gave unto him." Now that the Prodigal Son is out of money, he is also out of friends. He spent his inheritance liberally on and with these people thinking he was making "friends" with the "in" crown in this distant land, but they were not becoming his friends. They were just with him to see what they could get out of him. Persons who live in the "world," and are not shaped and influenced by Jesus, his Word, the Great Commandments, and the Holy Spirit often operate from a "what's in it for me" perspective. They frequently "use" other people in order to gain influence, access privileges, meet certain persons, or to get certain jobs, access money or goods, or for the ability to be presented with other opportunities or conveniences. This is one of the tough lessons the Prodigal Son learns as no one, among those who helped him spend his inheritance on wild living, will even give him animal feed to eat as he is literally starving to death in this distant and famine-stricken land.

When the Lights Come On

Sin obscures our perspective and hinders our spiritual sight. When we disobey God and travel to a foreign land where sin and disobedience abound, we will find that it is a land where things are not as they seem, promises are broken, persons are frequently selfish and unfaithful, and spiritual disease and spiritual death are prevalent. This is what Paul speaks of in Romans 6:23 where he states: "For the wages of sin is death; but the gift of God is eternal life through Jesus Christ our Lord." Sin causes things to die in our lives. It may not always be our physical bodies, but it may be the death of our integrity, character, hopes, dreams, marriages, and careers. And, as is the case with the Prodigal Son, sin and disobedience may bring the death of our family unity, our relationships with our parents, spouse, or children, our financial security, our physical and mental health, or our inspiration and enthusiasm. My Daddy, Mr. Herbert M. Allen, taught me the saying that: "There are fates worse than death." I remember not understanding when I was younger and thinking that it was one of those parents' perspective things. However, as I have lived for 54 years now, and been a Christian for 28 years, I came to realize that Daddy is correct that there are indeed fates that are worse than physical death. This particular essay doesn't afford me the time and space to thoroughly flesh out and defend this statement but suffice it to say that the loss of hope, purpose, faith, and love is indeed a fate worse than death. This perspective can be supported by the words of St. Paul in 1 Corinthians 13:13 where he proclaims: "And now abideth faith, hope, [love], these three; but the greatest of these is [love]."

The young man has a moment of clarity as he is feeding these pigs. He changes his focus, and the lights come on in his mind. He knows that the servants in his father's household have more than enough to eat. Notice, he is now "looking" at his father's house, and he is recognizing that even the servants there have it much better than he has in this foreign, sinful, and famine-stricken land. Just as sin begins in the heart and mind as we encounter temptation, holiness and obedience begins in the heart and mind as well. The Prodigal Son first looks back to his father's home in his mind's eye, and he subsequently chooses to turn around and begin his journey home to wear is mind's eye is looking.

Interestingly, this is the same process that he went through when he made the decision to ask for his inheritance, so he could run off to this distant land to live sinfully and waste "…his substance with riotous living" (Luke 15:13). He thought about and coveted in his mind's eye the fast living and heavy partying taking place in this foreign land, and his feet soon followed where his mind had gone. Repentance takes place in a very similar way. However, the big difference is that repentance is good and is always recognized and rewarded by God while sin is never good and brings God's judgment, chastening, and discipline.

The Prodigal Son's moment of clarity is evident in vv. 17-19 where we read:

> And when he came to himself, he said, How many hired servants of my father's have bread enough and to spare, and I perish with hunger! I will arise and go to my father, and will say unto him, Father, I have sinned against heaven, and before thee. And am no more worthy to be called thy son: make me as one of thy hired servants.

True repentance is a change of direction in heart, mind, and then action. God always recognizes, honors, and blesses repentance that is heartfelt, properly motivated, and is coupled with genuine remorse and contrition. Fake or inauthentic repentance accomplishes nothing because, although the actual sinful action make be eliminated in the eyes of man, the sinful heart and mind is still seen by God. And, the individual remains guilty of the sin if it remains in the heart and mind even if the sinful activity is eliminated. However, when we repent in heart, mind, and action, we put ourselves in a place where God can truly forgive, bless, and begin strengthening us to keep our commitment to holiness and living as citizens of his holy kingdom. This dynamic is evident in 1 Samuel 16:7 where we read: "…for the Lord seeth not as man seeth; for man looketh on the outward appearance, but the Lord looketh on the heart."

The reason the Prodigal Son begins being blessed as he turns his heart and mind to his father's house, and we are blessed as well when repentance begins in the heart and mind, is because we are now agreeing with God and seeing things as God sees them and not as our sinful and weak flesh sees things. This is in part what the apostle John speaks of in 1 John 1:9 where he states: "If we confess our sins, he is faithful and just to forgive us our sins, and to cleanse us from all unrighteousness." When we "confess our sins," we are agreeing with God that our sin is sin. We are no longer thinking it is "fun" or "exciting." On the contrary, when we "confess our sins," we are agreeing with God that sin is terrible, destructive, and it brings misery and pain into our lives as well as those around us. In other words, we have turned all of the lights on, and we are admitting our guilt and calling sin and disobedience what it really is. We are "confessing" to God what we have done wrong, and we are asking God to forgive us. In order for God to truly forgive us, we must have repented, and turned away, from the sin. God cannot forgive us if we "confess" only and do not repent, turn away from and forsake the sin because as soon as God forgives us we become guilty of it once again. However, if we "confess" our sins, and turn away from and forsake, our sins, God can truly forgive us. And, when he does, we are now in a "forgiven state." Our Roman Catholic friends call this the "state of grace."

The lights come on for the Prodigal Son when he decides he will turn away and "leave" the distant land, which is repentance, and he will "return" to his father's house. He also makes a commitment to abide by the standards and house rules, which is holiness, that are expected of even the servants who live in his father's house. This is evident in vv. 18-19 where he declares:

> I will arise and go to my father, and will say unto him, Father, I have sinned against heaven, and before thee. And am no more worthy to be called thy son: make me as one of thy hired servants.

In great humility, the Prodigal Son makes the decision to turn away from this sinful and wretched land and begin the long journey back to his father's house. Here, we see what genuine repentance looks like. It involves a complete change of direction in heart, thought, and deed. Knowing that he is guilty of many sins, including wasting his inheritance in this sinful land, the young man is willing to return home and be one of his father's servants. He will be thankful just to be blessed with the many blessings that the servants "in his father's house" enjoy.

In great humility, he recognizes that he no longer deserves to be called his father's "son," but he has faith that his father will receive him as one of his servants. This reminds us that faith plays a role in repentance and restoration. We must have faith that God will forgive us, and receive us, when we "confess" and truly repent of our sins and seek to be reconciled to him. Because God is good, and he celebrates when sinners return home to him, the Prodigal Son is quite surprised at the reception he receives as he approaches "his father's house." As we read this powerful part of the story, we are reminded that God's grace is truly amazing, and he loves us more that we can comprehend of understand. And, we see the truth of the words of Paul in Romans 5:20 where he proclaims: "…where sin abounded, grace did much more abound." And, the Prodigal Son sees what Paul speaks of in Ephesians 3:20 where he states that God "…is able to do exceeding abundantly above all that we ask or think, according to the power that worketh in us." Instead of being confronted with judgment when he gets home, the Prodigal Son is confronted with love, mercy, compassion, and forgiveness. The strength of the father's unwavering love trumps and overrides the younger son's sin and disobedience, and the younger son's confession, repentance, remorse, and return to his father's house put him in a place where restoration and reconciliation could become a beautiful reality in his life.

PART III -- RESTORATION

Chapter 3 – Waiting to Receive and Running to Forgive

Luke 15:20-23 – "And he arose, and came to his father. But when he was yet a great way off, his father saw him, and had compassion, and ran, and fell on his neck, and kissed him. And the son said unto him, Father, I have sinned against heaven, and in thy sight, and am no more worthy to be called thy son. But the father said to his servants, Bring forth the best robe, and put it on him; and put a ring on his hand, and shoes on his feet: And bring hither the fatted calf, and kill it; and let us eat, and be merry: For this my son was dead, and is alive again; he was lost, and is found. And they began to be merry."

The Enduring Love of the Father

The day the loving father has longed for has finally arrived. You see, he has waited and longed for his son's return for days on end. He has kept watch, waiting and wanting to look down the long road that leads to the house and sees his son coming home. He has envisioned it a hundred times, and he has prayed and asked God to bring his lost son home safe and sound. Day after day, he goes out to the front of the house and keeps vigil awaiting his son's return. He never misses a day, and his love for his disobedient son "Rejoiceth not in iniquity, but rejoiceth in the truth; Beareth all things, believeth all things, hopeth all things, endureth all things" (1 Corinthians 13:6-7). This father's love for his son has endured and continues to endure day in and day out, and this father's love exemplifies and represents God's great love for sinners like you and me.

Our loving heavenly Father awaits the return of prodigal sons and daughters, and he runs to embrace them and welcome them home when they repent and return to him. God is not like men who say "I told you so!" or "You should have listened to us!" No, there is no time for such speeches, and the father doesn't even allow the Prodigal Son to finish the speech he has prepared. There is no time for these speeches because there is too much to celebrate. And, the father must begin doing what a loving father who has longed for his son's safe return does; he must begin the joyful and celebratory process of welcoming the young man home and restoring him to his position in the family as the younger son. He begins restoring him to the same position he had prior to his departure to the foreign and sinful land.

The son hopes to be received as a servant and be able to live in his father's servants' quarters, but he is not received as a servant; he is received as a son. The love of this father for his son has weathered his son leaving him, requesting and spending the inheritance, disgrace and disrespect due to his son's immorality and indulgence in the distant land, and the shame and gossip his son's behavior brought to the family name in their community and town. This father's love trumps any concern about keeping up appearances, and he is not concerned about what his neighbors might say about his hasty and unconditional reception of his son. The one thing this man longed for, and prayed for, and hoped for, for days on end, from morning to noon to night, has become a reality on this unsuspecting, normal, and regular day, and it has now become one of the most glorious days in this father's life. He doesn't want to give or listen to speeches for it is time to celebrate and rejoice because his son, who was missing, is no longer missing. His son who was absent is now present, and was dead is now alive, and was lost is now found. (Luke 15:24)

Symbols of Restoration: A Robe, Ring, Shoes, and a Fatted Calf

The young man's father doesn't wait for his son to walk up the long road to the house, but he runs to his son and embraces him while he is still a long way from the house. Here, we see a portrait of God's amazing grace. In v. 20, we read: "And he arose, and came to his father. But when he was yet a great way off, his father saw him, and had compassion, and ran, and fell on his neck, and kissed him." God comes to us and loves us first. Jesus went to the cross before any of us were even born, so he loved us first. As this father runs to embrace his son, who has brought shame and dishonor to the family, we see the radical and unwavering nature of God's amazing grace and love. Through the major prophet Jeremiah, God tells us: "…Yea, I have loved thee with an everlasting love: therefore with lovingkindness have I drawn thee" (Jeremiah 31:3). And, the apostle John states it succinctly when he says: "We love him, because he first loved us" (1 John 4:19).

In the father's sprint to embrace his son, while his son is still a long walk from home, we see what we Wesleyan Christians call God's prevenient grace. This is God's grace that comes to us before we make it home to God's house and kingdom. Prevenient grace comes to us before we put our faith in the broken body and shed blood of Christ, and God comes to us way before we make our decision to worship and serve his Son, trust him as our Savior, and obey him as our Lord. Notice, the son is not home yet, but he is embraced by his father. Through prevenient grace, which is grace that comes before, God moves in our hearts and lives and steers us in the direction of home. And, when we get home, we like the Prodigal Son, find that we are embraced, loved, and restored by our loving heavenly Father. Then, we, like the Psalmist, can rejoice and celebrate the glorious truth that: "Surely goodness and mercy shall follow [us] all the days of [our lives]: and [we] will dwell in the house of the Lord for ever" (Psalm 23:6).

As his father embraces him, the son says in v. 21: "...Father, I have sinned against heaven, and in thy sight, and am no more worthy to be called thy son." Here, we see a genuine example of true repentance. Notice, the Prodigal Son confesses his sins, and he is willing to face the consequences of his sins. Since sin always brings consequences, he is prepared to no longer be a son, but he hopes to be one of his father's servants. He is willing to be content with being one of his father's servants because, with great remorse, contrition, and repentance, he knows he doesn't even deserve to be one of his father's servants. He knows his father will be showing a great amount of grace and mercy by making him one of his servants. When he "arose," in the foreign land and decided to return home to his father, he said to himself in vv. 18-19:

> I will arise and go to my father, and will say unto him, Father, I have sinned against heaven, and before thee, and am no more worthy to be called thy son: make me as one of thy hired servants.

The Prodigal Son demonstrates great contrition and humility, and he confesses and takes responsibility for his sins. He also shows by his actions that he has truly repented of his sins because he has left the foreign land and returned home to his father's house. If he is fortunate enough to be allowed to be one of his father's servants, he will be content and feel very blessed to abide by the rules laid out for the servants and to spend the rest of his life as a servant instead of a son. He knows he has forfeited his status as a son, and it will only be by his father's great mercy and grace that he "might" be received and allowed to be one of his father's servants. This young man's great humility reminds us of what James says in James 4:10 where he states: "Humble yourselves in the sight of the Lord, and he shall lift you up." And, we also see in this powerful story that God, like this father, "…is able to do exceeding abundantly above all that we ask or think, according to the power that worketh in us" (Ephesians 3:20).

As mentioned earlier, this joyful father isn't interested in tearful or judgmental speeches, and he doesn't say to the servants: "Prepare a room for our new servant in the servants' quarters." No. On the contrary, in vv. 22-24, the father says to his servants:

> ...Bring forth the best robe, and put it on him; and put a ring on his hand, and shoes on his feet: And bring hither the fatted calf, and kill it; and let us eat, and be merry: For this my son was dead, and is alive again: he was lost, and is found. And they began to be merry.

Notice, all of the things his father gives him in celebration of his homecoming distinguish the young man as a son instead of a servant. First, he instructs the servants to get one of the nice robes and to "put it on him." If he were a servant, he would not be allowed to wear one of these robes, and the servants would not be instructed to "put it on him." These robes were probably worn only by members of the immediate family, and these robes more than likely bear the family coat of arms, letters, and/or insignia.

Also, notice that the father instructs the servants to "...Bring forth the best robe, and put it on him;" (V. 22) The father doesn't call for just any of the family robes, but he calls for the "best robe" to be put on his son. Since it is this "best robe," it is very likely that it is the father's robe. The father is so happy his son is home that he allows him to wear the very best robe which is probably the father's own robe. This reminds us that when sinners truly repent, and return to God, his grace is amazing. And, he doesn't hesitate to welcome sinners home and allow them to have the very best things, and experience the most wonderful aspects, of living their new lives as citizens of his kingdom. Jesus emphasizes this glorious truth in Luke 12:32 where proclaims: "Fear not, little flock; for it is your Father's good pleasure to give you the kingdom."

This loving father also has his servants put a ring on his son's hand. Many believe that the ring also bore the family insignia, and the son's ability to stamp documents with the insignia on the ring, and conduct business for his father, is restored when he is given this ring. A servant would not be allowed to wear one of these rings. And, the father instructs his servants to put shoes on his son's feet. This also distinguishes him as a son, instead of a servant, because many believe that servants at that time didn't wear shoes. And, lastly but certainly not least, the joyful father calls for the fatted calf to be killed in preparation for a great celebration as the family rejoices and commemorates the return of the younger son. The killing and cooking of the "fatted calf" is only done for the most special of occasions, and the father is honoring his son by killing the "fatted calf" and throwing a great celebratory feast in order to rejoice and commemorate the return of his son. In. vv. 23-24, the father says:

> And bring hither the fatted calf, and kill it; and let us eat, and be merry: For this my son was dead, and is alive again; he was lost, and is found. And they began to be merry.

Like this loving father, God receives sinners when they repent, confess their sins, and return home to him. This son at this point in the story experiences something similar to what we Wesleyan Christians call justifying grace. Justifying grace is the grace that we enter into and experience when we first put our trust in the broken body and shed blood of Christ on the cross. When a sinner accepts Christ, believes the Gospel, and puts his or her trust in the atoning work of Christ on the cross, he or she is born again, receives the Holy Spirit, experiences regeneration, and is forgiven of all sins and received as a citizen in the kingdom of God. When the Prodigal Son returned home, instead of being made a servant, which is close to what he deserved, he is declared "not guilty" by his father, and he is "justified" by his father's grace, love, and mercy. A good way to remember what justifying grace is all about is to remember that it is when we trust in Christ, and are saved, and it is "just if I'd" never sinned.

Grace is the undeserved goodness, mercy, compassion, and forgiveness of God. The father treats and receives his son just as if he'd never sinned and left home to waste his inheritance partying and living sinfully in a foreign land. This is all behind him now, and his father has received and forgiven him. The very nature of forgiveness is to "forego" holding the person accountable for what they did. It is to give back resentment, the right to seek revenge or to retaliate, and the desire to see the person "pay" for what they did to us. The Parable of the Prodigal Son is one of the most celebrated and loved stories ever told, and we love it so very much because it promises us that our God forgives us when we repent and return home to him. He receives and forgives us, and we are "justified," and declared "not guilty," by our Judge as we enter into and experience God's amazing and justifying grace. The apostle Paul speaks of this amazing and justifying grace in Romans 5:1-2 where he states:

> Therefore being justified by faith, we have peace with God through our Lord Jesus Christ: By whom also we have access by faith into this grace wherein we stand, and rejoice in hope of the glory of God.

Because we are forgiven, and we stand in God's amazing grace, we are able to share and show God's grace, love, and mercy to others. The father of the Prodigal Son knew about grace and mercy, so he was able to extend it to his son even though his son squandered his inheritance, brought shame to the family, and lived sinfully in a foreign land. It is very likely that this father experienced radical forgiveness and unconditional love at some point in his life when he needed it, so he was familiar with and able to speak the language of forgiveness. So, when his son returns home, he is able to extend grace and forgiveness to his son because it is something that is not "foreign" to him. Learning to truly forgive others is in some ways like learning a foreign language. The language of forgiveness is not a language frequently spoken in our culture which focuses so heavily on results, performance, production, and accountability. Our flesh doesn't naturally lean in the direction of forgiveness; it is a language we must study and practice in order to speak it fluently. Forgiveness does not come naturally to us, but we learn it in our Spirits as we say "no" to our sinful flesh and "yes" to the teachings of our Lord who only provides additional commentary on one theological concept within the Lord's Prayer as he states:

> For if ye forgive men their trespasses, your heavenly Father will also forgive you: But if ye forgive not men their

trespasses, neither will your father forgive your trespasses. (Matthew 6:14-15)

We must speak the language of forgiveness to others if we want to be able to hear it and understand it when we need it. It is the height of hypocrisy to walk around, forgiven of all of your sins, and to hold something against someone and refuse to forgive them. When someone needs our forgiveness for a wrong perpetrated against us, we have an opportunity to obey and honor Jesus as our Lord. We have an opportunity to show someone the love and mercy we have received from God, and we have an opportunity to show the world, and to remind ourselves, that there is more to life than holding grudges, harboring resentment, and seeking revenge. There is a God who forgives us, and there is a Savior who died and rose again for us, and this God:

> ...so loved the world, that he gave his only begotten Son, that whosoever believeth in him should not perish, but have everlasting life. For God sent not his Son into the world to condemn the world; but that the world through him might be saved.
> (John 3:16-17)

PART IV – REJECTION

Chapter 4 – An Angry Older Brother

Luke 15:25-32 – "Now his elder son was in the field: and as he came and drew nigh to the house, he heard musick and dancing. And he called one of the servants, and asked what these things meant. And he said unto him, Thy brother is come; and thy father hath killed the fatted calf, because he hath received him safe and sound. And he was angry, and would not go in: therefore came his father out, and intreated him. And he answering said to his father, Lo, these many years do I serve thee, neither transgressed I at any time thy commandment: and yet thou never gavest me a kid, that I might make merry with my friends: But as soon as this thy son was come, which hath devoured thy living with harlots, thou hast killed for him the fatted calf. And he said unto him, Son, thou art ever with me, and all that I have is thine. It was meet that we should make merry, and be glad: for this thy brother was dead, and is alive again; and was lost, and is found."

The Sense of Religious Superiority and Judgmental Churchianity within the Church

Jesus had a particular issue with the Pharisees and others who were guilty of religious hypocrisy and self-righteousness. When we speak of the Pharisees, I think it is very important that we not paint with too broad a brush. Many of the Pharisees back in the first century were very devout and holy men who truly aimed to daily obey God by meticulously observing both the written and oral laws of Judaism. Nevertheless, some of them were religious only outwardly while inside their hearts were far from God. In Matthew 23:23-28, Jesus speaks about the hypocrisy of some of the scribes and Pharisees by stating:

> Woe unto you, scribes and Pharisees, hypocrites! for ye pay tithe of mint and anise and cumin, and have omitted the weightier matters of the law, judgment, mercy, and faith: these ought ye to have done, and not to leave the other undone. Ye blind guides, which strain a gnat, and swallow a camel. Woe unto you, scribes and Pharisees, hypocrites! for ye make clean the outside of the cup and of the platter, but within they are full of extortion and excess. Thou blind Pharisee, cleanse first that which is within the cup and platter, that the

outside of them may be clean also. Woe unto you, scribes and Pharisees, hypocrites! for ye are like unto whited sepulchres, which indeed appear beautiful outward, but are within full of dead men's bones, and of all uncleanness. Even so ye also outwardly appear righteous unto men, but within ye are full of hypocrisy and iniquity.

It appears that our very sweet, humble, meek, and mild Savior had no problem at all with calling out religious hypocrites who claimed to be holy while their hearts and minds were far from God and "…weightier matters of the law…" (Matthew 23:23) like mercy, compassion, faith, and love.

Jesus' consistent speaking out against the religious hypocrisy, and sense of religious superiority among the scribes and Pharisees, is also a factor in two of the three parables in Luke 15. The self-righteous scribe or Pharisee is represented in the "… over ninety and nine just persons, which need no repentance..." (Luke 15:7) in the Parable of the Lost Sheep. And, the self-righteous scribe or Pharisee is represented by the elder son in the Parable of the Prodigal Son who "...these many years [did serve his father and] neither transgressed [he] at any time [his father's] commandment..." (Luke 15:29). We know that Jesus is reprimanding the scribes and Pharisees in these verses because we are quite aware that there is nowhere on earth where we can find 99 men and/or women who need no repentance. One might say: "Perhaps we could find 99 just persons in a Monastery or Convent." No, we will not even find 99 just persons even in the holiest of religious communities where persons strive to live for and obey God daily throughout their entire lives. There is only one who needs no repentance, and he is the One telling the magnificent and brilliant parables of Luke 15. Similarly, there is no son or daughter who has obeyed his or her father always and never disobeyed his or her father. Once again, Jesus, the One who is without sin, and the One who is the Master Teacher continues his polemic against the hypocrisy of the scribes and Pharisees. And, he continues to have a significant problem with those who claim to follow him, yet only obey him outwardly with rituals and ceremonies, while their hearts harbor hatred, racism, greed, lust, selfishness, materialism, and all kinds of other sinful and wicked things.

I have recently become aware of the perfect word for what "Christians" who are only outwardly religious are practicing, and the word is Churchianity. Those who have never truly trusted in the atoning work of Christ on the cross, repented of their sins, accepted Jesus as their Lord and Savior, put their faith in Christ, and been born again are often counted among the "Christians" who practice Churchianity instead of Christianity. Those who are practicing Churchianity are only and overly concerned with the way things look, and there is very little concern about inward holiness and whether or not God's love is present within the heart. In Matthew 5:8, Jesus says: "Blessed are the pure in heart: for they shall see God."

The elder son in the Parable of the Prodigal Son thinks he has obeyed his father for many years and that he is close to his father. However, he is not. I speculate that much of the elder son's obedience to his father was done out of a sense of duty instead of love. It appears that he has secretly resented staying home and being a good and loyal son. Some

Christians wake up one day and find that they are in this same boat. We go to church and Bible Study, and we pray, worship, and read Scripture but find that somehow our outward religious acts of piety and devotion are somehow lacking or not inspiring and giving us the spiritual joy, peace, and satisfaction that they once did. When this happens to truly saved and born again Christians, I contend that chances are we have kept up our outward religious observances while letting our hearts drift away from God. This is the work of the devil who tries trick us into believing prayer, Scripture, and worship don't really matter, and they don't really change anything. However, the enemy can only prompt us to stop our outward observances of our faith if our hearts have already been lured away from the focus of our faith and devotions which is Jesus Christ our Lord and his eternal kingdom. We must be diligent and not allow this to happen by keeping Jesus and his kingdom first in our lives as Jesus teaches us to in Matthew 6:33 where he states: "…seek ye first the kingdom of God, and his righteousness; and all these things shall be added unto you."

The Self-righteous and Judgmental Elder Son

The elder son in the Parable of the Prodigal Son represents the self-righteous Pharisees and scribes Jesus rebukes in the parables in Luke 15. In Luke 15:1-3, Luke introduces the Parables by stating:

> Then drew near unto him all the publicans and sinners for to hear him. And the Pharisees and scribes murmured, saying, This man receiveth sinners, and eateth with them. And he spake this parable unto them, saying,

Here, we see that it was good "religious folk" who were criticizing and complaining about Jesus spending time eating with and reaching out to those they considered "sinners." Our humble and kind Savior had no problem at all with condemning the hypocrisy demonstrated by those who looked down on others while considering themselves to be holy. Self-righteous religious pride is a very serious sin, and the persons who have it are just as deceived as persons led astray by other sins of the flesh like hatred, lust, greed, drunkenness, and idolatry. In fact, in a list in Proverbs 6 of seven things that are an abomination to the Lord, pride is number one on the list. (Proverbs 6:16-19) God obviously has a serious issue with pride, and this is evident in multiple places in the Scriptures. The combination of pride and religion in the life and attitude of a sinful man or woman does not go over well with the God who bled and died, incarnate in the Jewish flesh of his Son our Lord Jesus Christ, to atone for our sins at the cross. Similarly, we honor Christ, and continue to recognize the enormity of what he accomplished in his crucifixion, when we never really lose sight of our immense sin debt which Jesus cancelled for us in his atoning work on the cross. The apostle Paul highlights this in Colossians 2:13-15 where he states:

> And you, being dead in your sins and in the uncircumcision of your flesh, hath he quickened together with him, having forgiven you all trespasses; Blotting out the handwriting of ordinances that was against us, which was contrary to us, and took it out of the way, nailing it to his cross; And having spoiled principalities and powers, he made a shew of them openly, triumphing over them in it.

No saved sinner should be "puffed up" thinking he or she is holier or better than any other Christian. One of the great benefits of salvation is recognizing how much we have been forgiven as a result of Jesus' death on the cross, and loving Jesus and others with an immense amount of love similar to the immense amount of sin that Jesus, our Savior, saved us from. Jesus loved sinners, and this is one of the main points in Chapter 15 of the Book of Luke. Jesus reached out to sinners and transformed their lives, and we will do the same if we truly love Jesus. No one is too far from God to be redeemed, forgiven, and transformed. This is part of the Gospel that sometimes doesn't go over well in contemporary society and among the overly religious and judgmental "Christians" in the church. It may not go over well with some of us "Christians" at times when murderers, thieves, robbers, and persons who have done other evil things repent, trust in Christ, return home to God, and are accepted by God within the church.

When this bothers us good "religious folk," and we murmur and complain that these former criminals are now our brothers or sisters in Christ, we are acting just like the elder brother in the Parable of the Prodigal Son. We better be glad murderers and thieves can be saved by trusting in the broken body and shed blood of Christ. If the blood of Christ couldn't atone for their sins, it would not atone for ours either, and no one could be saved. The apostle Paul highlights this in Romans 3:22-24 where he states:

> Even the righteousness of God which is by faith of Jesus Christ unto all and upon all them that believe: for there is no difference: For all have sinned, and come short of the glory of God; Being justified freely by his grace through the redemption that is in Christ Jesus:

It is true that sometimes murderers and thieves get truly saved and sometimes church going religious persons do not. It is all about the heart and whether or not Christ is enthroned there in the person of the Holy Spirit. Jesus emphasizes this in Matthew 21:31 where he declares: "Verily I say unto you, That the publicans and the harlots go into the kingdom of God before you."

As is often the case with the spiritually proud, the elder son is quick to stand in judgment of his younger brother. And, as he brags to his father about how "good" he has been, the elder brother also disrespects his father by refusing to celebrate the return of his brother, and he commits the sin of not honoring his father (Exodus 20:12), even as he proclaims that he has never disobeyed his father. As the elder son approaches the house, he hears music and dancing and asks a servant what the celebration is about. (Luke 15:25-26) Notice, the servant responds by saying: "...Thy [Your] brother is come; and thy [your] father hath killed the fatted calf, because he hath received him safe and sound" (Luke 15:27). Here, we see that the servant correctly refers to the elder brother's younger brother as "your brother." However, in his anger and in a disrespectful tone which shows what is in his heart, the elder son refers to his little brother as his father's son instead of as his brother. He dishonors his father by not receiving his brother back as his brother, and he doesn't share in his father's great joy that the Prodigal Son has returned home unharmed.

This demonstrates that the elder brother's heart is far away from his father's heart. And, I suspect, the elder brother resented staying home and carried out his duties due to a sense of obligation and social norms rather than out of his love for his father. His radical and obviously exaggerated concept of never disobeying his father denotes a pride in his good works and that he is keeping a tally of all the work he does around his father's house. In a religious context, good things done only out of a sense of duty and obligation, that lack the inward motives of love for God and neighbor, do very little to expand the kingdom of God. We must unite pure inward motives with good works in order to be truly obedient and to make a difference for Jesus and his kingdom.

True Christian discipleship involves the unity of faith in the heart and good works with the hands.

The apostle James speaks of this in James 2:17-18 where he says:

> Even so faith, if it hath not works, is dead, being alone. Yea, a man may say, Thou hast faith, and I have works: shew me thy faith without thy works, and I will shew thee my faith by my works.

Here, James makes the point that good works are a result of our faith. We do good works because we are saved not to be saved. Also, we do good works because God loves us and saved us and not to get God to love and save us. Those who are truly born again should hear alarm bells going off anytime they feel like they "deserve" something from God or that good works will lead us to better standing with God. Now, we all know that God does bless us when we love him and each other and do good things for others as a result of the faith and love within our hearts. It is only by God's grace that we sinners, no matter how obedient and holy, are able to walk and talk with a holy God and spend eternity with him from the day we trust in Jesus here on earth and on into eternity. The apostle Paul states this clearly in Ephesians 2:8-9 where he proclaims:

> For by grace are ye saved through faith; and that not of ourselves: it is the gift of God: Not of works, lest any man should boast.

The elder brother is demonstrating several aspects of hypocrisy by claiming to be a good son while not sharing his father's joy and referring to the Prodigal Son as his father's son instead of his little brother. We see this in Luke 15:28-30 where we read:

> And he was angry and would not go in: therefore came his father out, and intreated him. And he answering said to his father, Lo, these many years do I

serve thee, neither transgressed I at any time thy commandment: and yet thou never gavest me a kid, that I might make merry with my friends: But as soon as this thy son was come, which hath devoured thy living with harlots, thou hast killed for him the fatted calf.

He is blatantly and publicly disrespecting his father by questioning his father's decision to receive the Prodigal Son back as a son, instead of a servant, and he complains that the fatted calf is being killed in celebration of the Prodigal Son's return. In the elder son, we see the judgmental attitude and the works righteousness perspective of "religious folk" who are practicing Churchianity instead of Christianity. Those who view repentance and forgiveness from this perspective tend to believe that one must "deserve" to be forgiven or somehow "earn" his or her way back into the fold.

Grace by its very nature is "gift," and it cannot be earned. It is given by God, and, like any gift, it must be received. The fact that it must be received should not be confused with earning. Receiving is not earning, but it is accepting as a gift something that someone else has earned. Christ earned our forgiveness at the cross, and his broken body and shed blood has paved the way for sinners to return home to their father's house. We, like the Prodigal Son, do not deserve to be welcomed home and have our heavenly Father rejoice and celebrate our return. However, this is what happens every time a sinner repents, turns around, and arrives at home at his Father's house where "…goodness and mercy shall follow [him] all the days of [his] life: and [he] will dwell in the house of the Lord for ever" (Psalm 23:6).

Like the Pharisee who sees the sins of others but tends to overlook his own, the elder brother is not aware that he is disrespecting his father, disowning his brother, and refusing to celebrate something that is a great blessing from God which is the return of his brother safe and unharmed. Here, we see the selfishness that is oftentimes involved in cases of self-righteousness and religious superiority. Let us learn from the elder son's bad example. And, let us always celebrate that God loves and forgives sinners and runs to them to lift them up and welcome them home.

PART V – REWARD

Chapter 5 – The Benefits of Coming Home

Luke 15:31-32 – "And he said unto him, Son, thou art ever with me, and all that I have is thine. It was meet that we should make merry, and be glad: for this thy brother was dead, and is alive again: and was lost, and is found."

Celebrating Salvation and Second Chances

Whenever a sinner is saved by God's amazing grace, it is always a miracle made possible only by the broken body and shed blood of Christ. In the Parable of the Prodigal Son, the Prodigal Son represents us sinners, and the father represents God. The point of the story is that God receives sinners back home when they repent of their sins and return home to live obediently and thankfully in their father's house. Although the Prodigal Son has wasted his inheritance, he still has what he really needs in order to live a productive and holy life. He has his father's love and support. The Prodigal Son was hoping his father would receive him back as a servant and allow him to have a place in the servant's quarters. However, the fact that he was given a robe, a ring, and shoes makes it clear that he was received back as a son and not a servant. The ring probably has the family insignia on it and can be used to stamp and seal documents as the person wearing it carries out official family business. And, the robe probably bears the family insignia as well and is only worn by members of the family. And, servants did not wear shoes so the fact that he was given shoes indicates that he was received back as a son and not a servant.

All of us who enjoy living in our Father's house, which is the kingdom of God, are thankful that our God is merciful, forgiving, and offers second, third, fourth, and four hundred and forty-fourth chances. Unlike men and women, God never gives up on any one, and he is always willing to receive repentant sinners back home and offer them another chance at living and enjoying an abundant and holy life.

Our Faithful Father Forgives

We live in a world where untruth and unfaithfulness is around every corner, so we sometimes don't know how to understand and process the concept that God is completely faithful and completely truthful. In the Parable of the Prodigal Son, the perspective of this fallen world is evident in the "good times" and many "friends" the young man had in the foreign land as long as he had money to spend on these so called "friends." And, the perspective and approach of the world is evident in the fact that the only job he could get when he ran out of money was a job feeding pigs. This is a particularly harsh reality for a young Jewish man, or, maybe not, seeing as he didn't seem to be very religious at all. Perhaps God was speaking through this humiliating situation to remind the young man just how far he had fallen. It certainly wouldn't be the first time God spoke to a disobedient son or daughter through a trying and humiliating situation, and it certainly isn't going to be the last.

In all of this, we see God's great faithfulness. God could have just left the Prodigal Son there in the distant land broke, homeless, with no friends, and no money, doing the religiously "unclean" work of feeding the pigs. However, God speaks to the young man's heart and reminds him that his father's love is so great that even his father's servants have decent food to eat, comfortable bunks to sleep in, clothes to wear, and shelters over their heads. He decides to turn away from the foreign land and begin the journey home to his father's house. When he arrives, his father runs to meet him, and his father throws a great celebration. It is time to rejoice because the son who was lost is now found.

The faithfulness of God to forgive sins is evident throughout the Bible. The Scriptures make it very clear that God forgives repentant sinners. This is one of the main points in the Parable of the Prodigal Son. God loves and forgives sinners but sometimes "religious people" don't. In 1 John 1:6-10, the apostle John states:

> If we say that we have fellowship with him, and walk in darkness, we lie, and do not the truth: But if we walk in the light, as he is in the light, we have fellowship one with another, and the blood of Jesus Christ his Son cleanseth us from all sin. If we say that we have no sin, we deceive ourselves, and the truth is not in us. If we confess our sins, he is faithful and just to forgive us our sins, and to cleanse us from all unrighteousness. If we say that we have not sinned, we make him a liar, and his word is not in us.

Here, we see the importance of being on the same page with God. God forgives us when we repent because repentance leaves the sin in our rearview mirrors. When there is no repentance, God cannot forgive because the sin is still present, and we are still guilty of it.

The elder son shows us who we don't want to be as religious persons. We want to be able to celebrate with God when sinners are saved instead of thinking they are unworthy or undeserving of forgiveness and salvation. Like the elder son, we are always in the kingdom of God, and we are always in our heavenly Father's house. Everything that God has is ours, and we are always with God both now and forever. Just as the elder son now owns everything his father has, we are recipients of the good things of God as his forgiven sons and daughters by faith and divine adoption. Therefore, let us always remember to honor our heavenly father and celebrate with him whenever a sinner repents and returns home. And, let us celebrate here on earth remembering that Jesus says "…there is joy in the presence of the angels of God over one sinner that repenteth" (Luke 15:10).

Whosoever Believes

It is said that the ground is level at the foot of the cross. In other words, all persons stand before God initially as lost sinners in need of salvation, and we also sometimes stand before God as saved sinners in need of forgiveness and second, third, fourth, or four hundred and forty-fourth chances. Therefore, the Parable of the Prodigal Son is every Christian's story just as John 3:16 is every Christian's text. In John 3:16, Jesus says: "For God so loved the world, that he gave his only begotten Son, that whosoever believeth in him should not perish, but have everlasting life." These magnificent words spoken by our Lord highlight what the greatest reward is for prodigals who come home to God. Prodigal sons and daughters who repent of their sins, and come home to their Father's house, are forgiven of all of their sins and granted eternal life in the kingdom of God which is without end.

Another great reward that repentant sinners receive is abundant life in their Father's house with their millions of brothers and sisters in Christ. The repentant prodigal enjoys the blessings and status of being a son or daughter of God, and he or she is empowered and enabled not only to live a holy a life but also to enjoy living a holy life while walking and talking with almighty God, his Son, and the Holy Spirit, within the body of Christ which is the Church Militant on earth, and the Church Triumphant in heaven. The apostle Paul sums it up succinctly by stating: "For ye are all the children of God by faith in Christ Jesus" (Galatians 3:26). We thank God that the Parable of the Prodigal Son is every Christian's story who has repented of his or her sins and returned home to his or her loving heavenly Father who rejoices and celebrates his son or daughter's return.

This is the good news of the Gospel, and this is the good news in the Parable of the Prodigal Son. Our God loves us radically, and he longs for and, when we wander off into a foreign land of sin and disobedience, he patiently awaits our return. When we have spent all we have, and sin has beat us down and all but destroyed us, and we raise our hearts and minds and turn and look toward our Father's house, he is the One who inspires us to long for the joy and peace that comes from holy living and close fellowship with God. And, we find that God has given us the strength to stand up, turn around, with the land of sin and disobedience behind us, and we are inspired and empowered to begin the long journey back to our Father's house.

Like the Prodigal Son, we know we are unworthy to be given places of honor and leadership in our Father's house, so we are content to think that we might be able to be servants. When we arrive, we find that we indeed are servants in our Father's house. We are servants that carry Bishop's Staffs, wear stoles, fill pulpits, preach in stadiums, become missionaries to thousands in distant lands, build universities, teach in universities, operate on and save the lives of others, write best-selling books, become pastors, youth directors, Christian educators, soldiers, sailors, doctors, lawyers, nurses, entrepreneurs, or whatever God calls and equips us to be. And, it all begins with a single step in the direction of our heavenly Father's house.

Made in the USA
Columbia, SC
17 March 2025